THE POWER OF ONE ANOTHER

MICHAEL GURCZYNSKI
- ORDAINED MINISTER

THE POWER OF ONE ANOTHER

allelon

Café Cristo Ministry

John 13:34-35

"A new command I give you: Love one another. As I have loved you, so you must love one another. By this everyone will know that you are my disciples, if you love one another."

DEDICATION

As John's Gospel says in John 21:25 "If they were all written down one by one, I suppose that the whole world could not hold the books that would be written."

I too would say if I wrote down every name of those who have touched my life and helped in my growth, faith, and understanding of God's Word, the whole world could not hold the list.

So, to each of you from my past be you grandparents, parents, siblings, friends, or complete strangers who prayed for me and often before I knew I needed it.

And to those in my life for many years who have walked in faith with me through hard times and good times I give you thanks!

As well as those God has brought more recently in my life to become part of my family and for those he has called in a special place in my heart that I may do his will, I give thanks!

In all and to all I thank you for I am who I am first because of Christ and because of each of you, yes "One Another" and the Love we have for each other.

PREFACE

Early on in my Christian walk I was quite broken having become by way of divorce a single parent of 4 children spread out from 4 years of age to my oldest who had just entered college. Believe me, besides a bad marriage or as I should say a marriage where "One Another" was not our focus, I was messed up. You couldn't tell on the outside as I was fairly successful in my career and had been since my early 20's.

However, even though I loved my children and though we fought profusely and right out viciously I sought comfort in my work and in activities that when looking back I am not at all proud of! However, much of that is for another book so let me refocus and stay on track with the personal experiences that most align with the topic and intent of this writing!

So, as I began to grow in my newfound walk with Christ which began a bit before my now ex-wife and I initially separated. Once we did and I became a single father it did not take me long to realize just how dependent I would become on God and on others. But that transition from being an independent person who

PREFACE

thought I controlled my destiny did not come easy or overnight. The concept of being humble enough to accept help from others was perhaps one of the most difficult challenges I initially faced since as I alluded to, I had always provided quite well on my own. Or at least so it seemed! It was exceedingly difficult to receive help when offered and at first, out of the question for me to ask for it.

But the dynamics had changed; life would be different now and I found myself feeling by myself which led me to seek God even more. I thank the Lord that in part due to my children and God leading me to a good church, I much more quickly than I would have expected knowing myself embraced the importance of community. A real family of people just like me at different levels in their journey with God and people who became family. In time, I would learn as I embraced scripture and dove in deeper that the Gospel of Christ was not just a "One Another" Gospel but that Christ's plan for his followers was hinged on us being a part of something bigger than ourselves and while God certainly is bigger than us and our problems, I am referring to the body of Christ which he uniquely plotted out a plan centered on "One Another". A plan that prior to this revelation I as many who are living worldly lives would find to be idiosyncratic!

As I and my family grew in our church community, we began to serve. I could see the Lord's hand in so many ways and through so many people and the numbers increase by day. Better yet I could begin to see him

PREFACE

using me despite still being at a state where I viewed our little family as broken. But God in his infinite wisdom had brought just the right people into our lives to become a true extension of our family and began to use us to do the same for others who felt broken!

As a family we encountered the homeless, the lost, the broken and God brought many of these children of his into our lives to love, serve, and help. Even when we at times had not enough to tend to our own needs God still provided a way for us to bless these people and miraculously through the grace of the Spirit working in others made provision for us so we could make provision for others. A principle I learned incredibly early on that I was blessed to be a blessing though in all honesty I spent much of my life just blessing myself and my nuclear family.

Over time this "One Another" experience transformed our family into one that I no longer viewed as broken but one I viewed as God did. God did not see us broken but he saw us whole in him and through his providence he filled in the gaps with others who Loved and served us and others we loved and served! As time settled, I was even eventually able to return to my career where he again began to bless me with plenty for, I had learned that I was not the owner of my finances, my possessions, and even my children but rather the steward of these blessings and gifts and He in fact was the owner.

While all credit is due to the voluntary sacrifice of our Lord and Savior as I began writing this book Easter

PREFACE

week of 2021, it had become abundantly clear that his plan which I refer to in the book's title as the "Power of "One Another" had been exactly what we had needed and clearly by what we are going to discuss in this book you will begin to see just how much emphasis our Savior and his disciples placed on our needs for each other. God's Word not only tells his Love story for us but the Love story he wants his Children to have is a Love story for "One Another". He desires us to be interdependent as the body of Christ, a mutual and healthy need of each other.

The experiences I shared so far with you, and will throughout this book only capture a glimpse of the mountains Jesus moved through his grace and the family of God he placed in our lives. Along with many years in the Word and those experiences is what has led me to write this book on the Power of the Greek Word *alleon* or in English the Phrase "One Another". Just the mere fact that Jesus and his disciples used the word alleon in the Holy Bible so frequently to instruct us as Christians how to and how not to treat "One Another" just simply cannot be overlooked without ignoring the wisdom left for us in the New Testament.

I pray this book blesses you as much as the time I spent studying God's Word and the movement of the Holy Spirit that went into this book are experienced by all who read. May the God of all Mercy, Grace, and Wisdom bless you and show you his plan through our willingness to embrace his "One Another" Gospel" and plan for Christian living!

CONTENTS

1 — Introduction
1

2 — Allelon - Greek for "One Another"
6

3 — The Themes of "One Another"
9

4 — Living In Unity as Christ Lives In Union with Us
22

5 — The Four Types in the Love Theme
25

6 — Humility & Servanthood
32

7 — Encouragement & Edification
36

8 — "One Another" Don'ts
60

9 — Christian Living Summed Up As "One Another"
63

INTRODUCTION

God's plan for mankind since the Garden of Eden has always been for us to be in relationship with Him and with our brothers and sisters. When we part from this earth and go to the place that Jesus has prepared for us, while there will be many rooms, there will only be two things other than God! That is right, two things, his Word and his Children which is why I like the phrase: "All we take from this world when we return to our true home in Heaven is relationships!"

We do not take our mansions, assuming you had one here on earth but for most folks our homes, our cars, our boats, our jewelry, our furniture, our money and so many other things we hold onto so dearly here on earth! As Jesus said in John 6:27: "*Do not work for food that spoils; instead, work for the food that lasts for eternal life. This is the food which the Son of Man will give you, be-*

cause God, the Father, has put his mark of approval on him."

And as the scriptures go, the crowds whom Jesus miraculously fed the day before had followed Him to Capernaum the next day but were seeking him for earthly things not what he had truly offered them the day before. While the signs and wonders he performed when he fed the 5000 had a purpose like giving testimony to whom he was to all through the miracle he had performed, the people much like the Pharisees simply just did not see the truth that was right in front of them. But rather then following him as he was calling the lost to follow him, they were seeking entertainment and free food as John testifies in his Gospel in John 6:26 where Jesus answered, *"I am telling you the truth: you are looking for me because you ate the bread and had all you wanted, not because you understood my miracles."*

Christ was not seeking mere popularity or to be an entertainer, nor was he seeking to be a physical King of this world as many were believed is what the scriptures promised. But rather Jesus had come to save us from our sins and while he walked with us on earth, he led us by example. Through his life, punishment, death, burial, and resurrection, he showed us the greatest Love story ever told, he willingly gave his life as the ransom for the sins that you and I were guilty of and the sins yet to come for all mankind.

So here in John's account and the other 3 Gospels' Jesus continues to clarify that the point of His ministry is spiritual, not material or as he says over and over "My Kingdom is not of this World". Scripture is consistent in reminding us that we need more than just physical food in order to thrive—we need to be nourished spiritually, as well (Isaiah 55:2; Matthew 4:4). Now, this does not mean our working has no value or that Jesus is endorsing laziness or in fact not eating as that would contradict the message the Bible carries on our bodies being the temple of the Holy Spirit.

On the flipside, Jesus' message is simply that all material things will eventually pass away. They will perish as a broken limb of a tree slowly turns back into the earth! Instead of being consumed with things like food and perishable things, we ought to be concerned with eternal rewards first and foremost.

So, you may be asking what all this has to do with the title of this book "One Another"? Well, the answer is everything because what Jesus also taught us was that while our physical bodies would indeed perish, he taught us that our Love for "One Another" when he said, "'Love the Lord your God with all your heart and with all your soul and with all your strength and with all your mind; and, Love your neighbor as yourself" in Luke 10:27. So again, relationships would be the only thing that went with us we were called home to be with God the Father, God the Son, and God the Holy Spirit.

With this being the case, and the fact that Jesus himself spoke intently on "One Another" and just hours before his persecution left us with a New Command in

John 13:34 where he says: "*And now I give you a new commandment: love "One Another". As I have loved you, so you must love "One Another". If you have love for "One Another", then everyone will know that you are my disciples*", the very essence of this statement should challenge us to seek more God-honoring relationships now and that was paramount in Jesus' plan for those who would follow him.

I enjoy such pleasure at the depiction of the early Church when I read the book of Acts. The early Church in Jerusalem had a level of oneness that was transformative. What marked their community was the willingness of each member to live selfless lives. Their commitment to follow Jesus' command to Love "One Another" was demonstrated in the real world.

Instead of each looking out only to meet their own needs, they shared their material possessions and resources with each other so that "there was not a needy person among them as documented in Acts 2:43-47. What a tremendous testimony and a beautiful depiction of what it would be if on the whole our Churches of today had the same heart for true oneness. Then perhaps it could too be said about us that our Love was seen by all for "One Another", and the Lord added to their numbers daily.

In my own personal experience, I have seen glimpses of the early Church through close knit relationships with my brothers and sisters in Christ in my many years attending and serving in my former Church in Florida.

As I grow in my maturity in Christ the yearning to let God lead me in a direction to build true Christian community heightens and he has paired me with another who has the same heart and together with God's help and our unique gifts we long to see a vision through that will resonate the very character of "One Another" in our modern world. However, further details on that vision are still in being revealed and being worked out and it is not yet time to share what has been written on our hearts says the Lord in his still small voice.

ALLELON - GREEK FOR "ONE ANOTHER"

Well by now you may be catching on to what this book is about! But you may be wondering why an entire book on the foundation of community? If you are not, in either case I am sure you will be equally as amazed as I was on what I am about to share with you on Biblical topic of community and how much it is emphasized throughout the Bible.

With that said, the phrase "One Another" is derived from the Greek word *allelon* which means "One Another" and in parallel the reference to "Each Other"; and how these references and often commands are mutually reciprocal." So, if you were not catching on to the thematic direction and purpose of my writing this book so far, I am confident that as you begin to dive in and grasp the very power and essence of Love that exist in Christian community you will see why this author found it worthwhile to write an entire book on this emphasis of oneness.

But hang on as there is much to share yet on the Greek Word *allelon*. The phrase in English translated from this single Greek word occurs 100 times in 94 New Testament verses. If that is not enough occurrence lets add that approximately 59 of those occurrences are specific commands teaching us how our Christianity is to be lived out and how it is not as a "One Another" body of believers.

Obedience to those commands is imperative and we will look at them in greater detail later in this book. For now, let us focus on just how the phrase "One Another" forms the very basis for true Christian Community, and has a direct impact on our witness to the world as described in John 13:35 where we again revisit this scripture as John quotes Jesus himself saying; "*If you have love for "One Another", then everyone will know that you are my disciples*". Due to the emphasis made by Christ himself and being it was one of the few words spoken by Jesus on the night he was to be taken into custody by the Temple Guards I think it is fair to assume on that basis alone it warrants our attention!

In addition to allelon, the Bible uses other words and phrases to instruct us how to relate to others. How to treat our brothers and sisters in Christ and a tough one for most of us how to treat our enemies. However, this book primarily focuses on the use of allelon, and while we may inherently touch on some other parallel phrases, words, and principles that relate you will find we have our work cut out for us just homing in on the various uses of "One Another" and the pivotal role this phrase or Greek word has in the day-to-day activities of our Christianity!

Now again while this book is primarily focused on the Greek Word Allelon or the English Phrase "One Another", many references to brother and sister in Christ or as the Bible refers to as brethren exists and that word stems from the Greek Adelphos (adelphoi). Brethren is used in the New Testament some 346 times. It is where we get our word "Philadelphia" (phileo = love, adelphos = brother). Yes, though it may not live up to its name the City of Philadelphia was named to be known as the city of brotherly love.

I will bet you might not have ever really thought of the word brethren or when we say brother or sister that its meaning is implicitly from the inspired Word of God in the Bible meant to mean Brotherly Love or be an expression of Love towards a brother or sister in Christ! Now that is an interesting fact and one that I believe ties in nicely with the theme of this book "POWER OF "ONE ANOTHER"!

THE THEMES OF "ONE ANOTHER"

There are both Positive and Negative contexts for the phrase "One Another". Essentially the positive can be broken down into four themes, with each theme collectively accounts for a proportionate percentage of the "One Another" lifestyle attributes. Coincidence? Probably not as our God is at minimum very intentional. So, this writer chooses to believe the balance we see in these four themes to be intentional and a part of God's providence and design for Christian living. These themes or grouping will help us later to see how God's divine providence has given us a guidebook to Christian Living and attached a great deal of it to the Greek word *allelon* or in English, the phrase "One Another"!

In this chapter we will surface these themes and in later chapters dive in much deeper with scripture, commentary and practical application from my own experiences in walking with the Lord for over 25 years. So, let us begin and start with Unity!

UNITY

The first of these themes deals with words like living in accord, agreement, harmony, unity or to sum it up how the Church is getting along and should be getting along! For example, we are to *"Seek good for "One Another", and don't repay evil for evil"* as instructed in 1 Thessalonians 5:15. And we are and by the way both if these are commanded; to *"Be of the same mind with "One Another"* as in Romans 12:16 and 15:5.

John Stephen Piper is a theologian, pastor, and chancellor of Bethlehem College & Seminary. Let us look at a segment of a sermon he ministered in 1988 and the Pastor of Bethlehem Baptist Church in Minneapolis, Minnesota!

Christian Unity and the Cross (Sermon)

January 24, 1988

1 Corinthians 1:10–17

For many years I have heard the saying: if two people think the same way about everything, one of them is unnecessary. It is usually quoted regarding marriage as a way of pointing up the enriching value of differing opinions between a husband and wife. And usually, the possibility of total agreement is pictured as boring.

The Sweetness of Christian Unity

I think I first heard this saying when I was in high school 25 years ago. I can remember thinking that it was clever but wrong. I still think it is wrong. If total agreement between two persons makes one of them unnecessary, then God the Son is unnecessary to God the Father and the fellowship of the Trinity is boring. Not only that, if total agreement between persons is boring, then heaven will be boring, and my perfected fellowship with Christ will be boring, and the camaraderie of like-minded friends in this world is boring, and the sweetest moments of blended minds in marriage are boring.

But we know from Scripture, and we know from experience that this is not so. Psalm 133 says,

> Behold, how good and pleasant it is
> when brothers dwell in unity!
> It is like the precious oil upon the head,
> running down upon the beard,
> upon the beard of Aaron,
> running down on the collar of his robes!
> It is like the dew of Hermon,
> which falls on the mountains of Zion.

The point of that psalm is the preciousness and sweetness of harmony and oneness and like-mindedness in the fellowship of God.

And I know from experience that the sweetest and deepest moments of fellowship in my life are the hours of relishing some great vision together with people who have the same convictions about God and about the world. And the deeper the agreement, the deeper the joy and the power of those moments.

PIPER JOHN (1988). *CHRISTIAN UNITY OF THE CROSS.* SERMON

LOVE

And of course, LOVE as not only the author and finisher of our faith but Jesus himself was the first in the New Testament to use the phrase "One Another"! In fact, as discussed before he commanded us to "Love "One Another"! While there may be some variance on this that I am not aware of in different translations, the command "Love "One Another" appears eleven times in the Bible, and all in the New Testament. Jesus is recorded as saying it three times. Twice in John 13:34 and once in John 13:35.

But who knows after all John himself quotes in his Gospel John Chapter 21 and verse 25 saying, *"Jesus did many other things as well. If every one of them were written down, I suppose that even the whole world would not have room for the books that would be written."* So perhaps while the context of the verse seems to be talking about miracles it is likely he emphasized "Loving One Another" more times than recorded.

Now keep in mind that when Jesus told his disciples to love "One Another" he said to do it "As I Have Loved You". That is a tall order and we as disciples are called to honor that same Command if we are to truly be his disciples! And speaking of command, the word command in the original Greek means an injunction, ordinance, or law. Jesus was not only summoning with an authoritative order, but he was also instituting a new law to replace the Law of Moses with the law of Love.

And if that is not enough a similar phrase "Love Each Other" is used in the same context and appears four times in the Bible, all in the New Testament. And again... Jesus said it twice, once in John 15:12 and once in John 15:17.

So again, I turn to snippet of a sermon by John Stephen Piper, theologian, pastor, and chancellor of Bethlehem College & Seminary, and former Pastor of Bethlehem Baptist Church in Minneapolis, Minnesota! I think what he shares augments this writer's thoughts in a very complimentary way.

"A New Commandment I Give You"

The verse that I want to focus on is John 13:34: "A new commandment I give to you, that you love "One Another": just as I have loved you, you also are to love "One Another". There are glorious things in verses 31–35 that

I am passing by. We will be back, Lord willing. Today there is only time for one verse and one question: *What is new about the commandment to love each other?*

I pray that Jesus himself will speak in this message concerning his commandment to Bethlehem that we love each other. Immerse your mind now in this text with me and let the mind of Jesus saturate your mind. That is how we are changed. The word of God reveals the Son of God and the glory of God by the Spirit of God, and we are changed (2 Corinthians 3:18). This a miracle. If I did not believe in it, I would not be a preacher of this word. It has power far beyond mine.

Christians Are Under Authority

John 13:34: "A new commandment I give to you, that you love "One Another": just as I have loved you, you also are to love "One Another". If you are a follower of Jesus, a Christian, a child of God through faith in Christ, you are a person under authority. You are not your own. You do not call the shots anymore. Jesus is more to you than Master of your life, but he is not less. He comes to you with more than commandments, but not less. You are a person whose life is defined by the will of another, namely, Jesus. What he wills you want.

And what he wills and commands in this verse is that we love each other—that his followers love each other. "A new *commandment* I give you"—not a new suggestion, or a new idea, or a new possibility, or a new life-option, but a new commandment.

What's New About Jesus' New Commandment?

The question that has guided all my focus in this message is *What is new about the commandment to love each other?* "A *new* commandment I give to you, that you love "One Another". I see two answers implied in this verse. The key to the answers is found in the words in the second half of the verse: "... just as I have loved you, you also are to love "One Another". The newness of the command to love each other is found in the words "as I have loved you."

I see two ways that the commandment to love each other is new in those words. First, the command is new because it is a command to *live out* the love of Jesus. Second, the command is new because it is a command to *live on* the love of Jesus. The words "as I have loved you" contain a *pattern* for our love for each other, and they contain a *power* for our love for each other.

Loving each other is not a new command *per se*. It was already there in the Old Testament (Leviticus 19:18, "You shall love your neighbor as yourself"). What is new is that Jesus is now the pattern we *live by* and the power we *live on*.

PIPER JOHN (2008). *THE NEW COMMANDMENT OF CHRIST: LOVE "ONE ANOTHER" AS I HAVE LOVED YOU*. SERMON

HUMILITY & SERVANT HOOD

Humility really hits home with excitement this morning as I sit at the keyboard sharing the importance of the phrase "One Another" with you! Not because it is of more importance than the other's but because I had recently as of this writing been asked by someone whom I was mentoring what being humble really meant! Frankly, I muttered through some examples but really did not in my opinion let the Spirit of God speak through me on the very topic I would begin just the next day in this book and one I had lived out and ministered on so many times before!

I woke to my devotions for the day being Philippians Chapter 2 verses 1-11 and subtitled in the Good New Translation "Christ's Humility and Greatness"! In just those 11 short verses which I will share with you in a moment there were three, yes three "One Another" references. They were:

1. "Have Compassion For One Another"
2. "Be Humble Toward One Another"
3. "Look Out For One Another's Interests"

As I pondered on this verse, I could feel the Spirit of God revealing the answer to me in my very studies and the words I am sharing with my readers was a more refined view on what being humble meant! In what I was learning lied the answer to the question my endeared friend asked. And that was that in God's economy being humble was not just merely doing without or living impoverished conditions because you gave all your money away.

Yes, the in the Gospels Jesus did ask the "Rich Young Ruler" to leave all his wealth behind, but that was what he needed to do to follow Jesus. But that is not what God calls each of us to do. Just think, if all Christian's were called to give up all they had, their homes, the cars, their money we would certainly not look to be a very appealing witness in the eyes of the unsaved. If this were the case, then how would the physical Church carry on? How would Outreach happen? How would we take care of Widows and Orphans as commanded in the Bible? How would we move the Gospel the way we do if we were all broke?

Yes, there is no doubt that much wealth exists that is not used for Kingdom purposes, and sadly that includes believers and unbelievers alike. However, what I am about to reveal as this writer's view on what Jesus calls us each to you should be able to see how my answer impacts both the misuse and incorrect thinking of those who view their time, talent, and treasures as theirs.

So, while Jesus may call on each of us to leave something behind to follow him to this writer's the answer to the question of "What being Humble Looks Like" is the act of applying the command of "One Another" and acknowledging our source Jesus Christ in all things no matter what they are and to do all things as unto the

Lord and for the sake of the Church by which I mean the brethren or my brothers and sisters as well as being trained up and training up disciples.

As you will see in Philippians Chapter 2 verses 1-11, I can say this with confidence because as Paul describes Jesus in this most humble passage that follows the principles, I just shared radiate with Humility as did the life, death, and resurrection of our Lord Jesus Christ.

Philippians 2:1-11

Your life in Christ makes you strong, and his love comforts you. You have fellowship with the Spirit, and you have kindness and compassion for "One Another". I urge you, then, to make me completely happy by having the same thoughts, sharing the same love, and being one in soul and mind.

Do not do anything from selfish ambition or from a cheap desire to boast, but be humble toward "One Another", always considering others better than yourselves. And look out for One Another's interests, not just for your own.

The attitude you should have is the one that Christ Jesus had: He always had the nature of God, but he did not think that by force he should try to remain equal with God. Instead of this, of his own free will he gave up all he had and took the nature of a servant. He became like a human being and appeared in human likeness.

He was humble and walked the path of obedience all

the way to death— his death on the cross. For this reason, God raised him to the highest place above and gave him the name that is greater than any other name.

And so, in honor of the name of Jesus All beings in heaven, on earth, and in the world below will fall on their knees, and all will openly proclaim that Jesus Christ is Lord, to the glory of God the Father.

ENCOURAGEMENT & EDIFICATION

As members of the body of Christ and true followers of Christ we are especially called to come alongside "One Another" to encourage and edify! Let us look at the act of Baptism first. Many think it is one dimensional as far as people are concerned with the person being Baptized making their public proclamation to God that they have decided to follow Jesus which is a partial truth!

By that I mean the act of Baptism in my years under sound teaching and time in the Word of God understanding our accountability to "One Another" makes Baptism multidimensional, meaning that we the Church are not just hearing the person being baptized testimony and proclamation, but we are too proclaiming to stand by their side as new believers and Encourage & Edify them that they are built up in their faith and stay on the straight and narrow path!

In my own life my Baptism was witnessed by 600 plus people, many who knew me as I was a ministry leader in the Church but of more importance in the context of accountability about 15% whom belonged to my inner circle. I did not just make a proclamation that day to profess Jesus as my Lord and Savior, I also looked to those brothers and sisters in Christ to hold me to be accountable in my walk and come along side me to grow in the things of the Lord.

Now with that also came the expectation of correction. As believers we are called to gently correct "One Another" when we see a brother or sister headed in a direction of error that would lead to sin. We are to be accountable to "One Another" and in order to do that we must embrace a "One Another" mindset in order to be less private and more vulnerable! In other words, to be willing to bring things out of the dark and into the light. Of course, we need to use discernment and wisdom to not get caught in a closeness that can be dangerous because the doors of the Church are not exempt from evil and people that long to bring us harm or deception!

However, that aside we should be concerned when we see a brother or sister not attending Church as they regularly do! When we see anti-patterns or for those not familiar with that phrase abnormalities in one's behaviors, we as the body ought to reach out be it phone, mail, or perhaps in person if we have a close enough relationship!

But in any case, we should also be praying for them and if we do not have a way to check in on them, call to the elders of the Church and the Church should reach out as in principle that is what the Word of God exemplifies by principle should be done.

CHAPTER 4

LIVING IN UNITY AS CHRIST LIVES IN UNION WITH US

God wants his Children to work together, as is displayed throughout the Bible and especially in many of the "One Another" scripture verses! You could say God wants us to work as a team or as the Bible refers to Unify as the physical body needing to work together and maintain a healthy and balanced life! A healthy interdependent relationship with those in our circles of influence and of like faith.

When individuals work together, they can double their strength and get much more done as a team. As my paraphrase of the scripture a threefold cord is not easily broken goes, there is greater strength in numbers. By living in Unity, we as Christians also reap the value of having worked in unison, thus creating harmony instead of disorder. Working as one people begins with the efforts of each person, as they work with "One Another".

I think back to my many years as a Servant Leader over what was referred to as Computer Check in but by more descriptive definition was using our Church management system to securely register children into children's Church each week. While there was a hierarchy as there is in a marriage, a Church, and most non dictatorship regions of the world, the team I led consisted of 50 and upwards of 60 volunteers all working in unison to achieve a smooth and secure process for God's Children. We were like family for we were family as we served together each week.

And our service did not stop there, in fact our service to "One Another" was equally vital to serving the congregation. As a leader I needed to foster into my Team Leaders a Love and concern for each of their team members. When one of us hurt we all hurt, when one of us was slipping we all stepped up and prayed and mentored. And when one was missing for a while, we did not get upset we became generally worried and did what was in our power to follow up and check in on them.

And why is this so important you may ask? Well at its simplest because we are all important to God and because in His Word, he has given us direction on what it means to live in Unity with "One Another"? Let us start with what Jesus has to say in the Gospel of John in Chapter 15 verses 5-8!

John 15:5-8 5

"I am the vine; you are the branches. If you remain in me and I in you, you will bear much fruit; apart from me you can do nothing. If you do not remain in me, you are like a branch that is thrown away and withers; such branches are picked up, thrown into the fire and burned. If you remain in me and my words remain in you, ask whatever you wish, and it will be done for you. This is to my Father's glory, that you bear much fruit, showing yourselves to be my disciples."

And when we live in Unity with Christ, we as he set the example are compelled and commanded to live in Unity with "One Another"! We are called to be at peace with, to be of the same mind, to accept, to gently, patiently tolerate, be kind, tender-hearted, and forgiving, to bear with and forgive, and to seek good for "One Another".

These are just a handful of the commands we are given directly by our Lord or through the inspired Word of the Apostles on how to live as one. To live and operate in Unity! To let Christ be Lord of our Lives and let that be evidenced by the Unity, which is founded on Love, our next Chapter that we have for "One Another".

CHAPTER 5

THE FOUR TYPES IN THE LOVE THEME

The empathetic style of communication in the bible and in Jesus's own words to "LOVE ONE ANOTHER" occurs numerous times throughout the gospels and the epistles.

As we discussed earlier Jesus Himself speaks of the importance of LOVE in John 13:34-35 which we will read in the text that follows; *"And on the night, he was to be taken captive by the Temple Guards He was focused on LOVE and not only then but all the way to the cross."* This verse really intrigues me in knowing that I personally have yet to meet a person, nor believe I or you ever will meet someone who in the midst of facing what Jesus was about to endure and knew it, would have acted the way he did or focused on the things he said to his disciples teaching them what to teach those that would follow them all the way to us and those yet to hear the Gospel of Christ thousands of years later and up until the Lord returns.

But even still he was focused on washing the feet of his disciples to set an example of servanthood. He was setting the Apostles up for their discipleship in emphasizing community and power through the command of Love just as he ministered to them in Word and action on the night of his arrest. At the cross he even took interest in his deepest time of suffering and perhaps minutes away from his final surrender to life and his last breath that His mother would be cared for by the Apostle John after he had gone and did so in agony but with Love, Joy, and Compassion for her as he uttered into your hands, I commit my Spirit to his Father God.

But then again Jesus was no ordinary person for he was God in the flesh, the Messiah, the King of Kings, The Great I am and the Name above all names! Yet we must also not lose sight in that he was a man, and this was not a task he was able to just divinely make easier for himself. Now don't get me wrong and I know this can be difficult at times for some to grasp or if we are being honest for all of us to grasp at one time or another; but Jesus was fully God and fully Man. Not half God and half man, not 80/20, not 40/60, but 100/100 yet he surrendered his divinity placing all trust in the Father as we were taught through his example to place all our trust in Him to be the propitiation for our sins, appeasing and gaining the favor of God whom he was but through the Father while facing every temptation, emotion, and fiber of life that you and I do each and every day.

In John 13:34-35 Jesus does not just follow the "Prefer "One Another", the "Love "One Another", or the "Serve "One Another", but in the window of time right before his hour of distress where he literally sweat blood in the Garden of Gethsemane, Jesus gave this New Command and I might say his adding "*As I Have Loved You*" set the bar extremely high considering the Love he was about to endure on what we now call Good Friday was a Love unlike any other that mankind had ever actually seen manifested in the flesh of a person because it was the Love of God, the pure essence of being Love and the manifestation of Love in the heavenly host!

And in the Epistle's John correlates the truth of our professed relationship with God metaphorically but at the same time literally with our Love for "One Another"! Even going as far as to say that; "*Whoever claims to love God yet hates a brother or sister is a liar. For whoever does not love their brother and sister, whom they have seen, cannot love God, whom they have not seen.*" His words, not mine but he certainly did not waste time at all in his three short letters which illustrate comparative principals and the same foundation of Love that Christ spoke of before he journeyed to the cross and the Love he demonstrated on the cross and through his death, burial and resurrection as we see in the following text from John's Gospel.

John 13:34-35

34 "A new command I give you: Love "One Another". As I have loved you, so you must love "One Another". 35 By this everyone will know that you are my disciples if you love "One Another".

Yes, even in his final hours, Jesus was still teaching and right to the last minutes he was still setting examples for his followers which explains much including why we see the phrases "LOVE ONE ANOTHER", and similar phrases such as "LOVE EACH OTHER DEEPLY" in 1 Peter 4:8 or "BE DEVOTED TO ONE ANOTHER IN LOVE" in Romans 12:10.

Unlike the English language where we Love hotdogs, we Love our wives, we Love our car, and so forth, in the bible derived from both the Greek and Hebrew there are 4 types of love expressed. So, the Bible is so much more precise on Love and sadly in the English language and in our attitudes and belief systems which are polluted with worldly views we are so limited in our understanding of Love and our ability to truly grasp, receive and give the kind of Love Jesus died for.

So, let us look a Love and take heart and appreciate just what Love means and Love is in the various context of the bible! But in any case, one thing that holds true for all context of the word Love is that Love is an action yes, a verb. It is intentional and giving not automatic and self-seeking.

ERŌS

The first type of Love is called erōs, which refers to Love you would expect to see between couples and is a Love that is romantic or sexual in nature.

STORGĒ

The second type of Love is storgē which refers to the kind of Love you have for a family member like the love between a parent and child or brothers and sisters.

PHILÍA

The third is philía, which refers to love you would have for people close in your life like close friends and would typically be referred to as the friendship love.

AGÁPĒ

But the fourth and the purest of loves is agápē, which is unconditional love, the kind of LOVE that God loves with, the kind of love that led Jesus to freely make his journey to the cross. It is a sacrificial Love and a Love we are called to have for "One Another" based on John 13:34 where Jesus concludes this verse with as I have loved you!

When Jesus commands us to love "One Another" as He loved us, He wants us to demonstrate an unconditional agápē love towards each other. But how do we do this on our own? Simply put we cannot. Even Jesus while he walked this earth needed regular communion with the Father and often went off for hours to pray!

You see when we are in fellowship with God and the Holy Spirit resides in us and we are walking in union with Christ then we can exhibit unconditional or **agápē love**. Will we exhibit this flawlessly, of course not or at least not on this side of heaven but with regular connection with God and the Holy Spirit dwelling within us as Jesus said "We will do even greater things"

While some may take this which is said by Jesus in John 14:12 as we would be able to perform miracles, walk on water, raise the dead, and teach and no less do it greater than Jesus! This is not at all what I believe Jesus spoke about and I confidently say this by the testimony in the Epistles of what the Apostle's did and it started with "Love "One Another" which Jesus said would be how they, meaning the lost would know we were his!

So greater things are more likely associated with more the work of Jesus of Loving as he did, testifying on his behalf because of what he did in front of them and the examples in his short ministry all the way up unto the cross that he left them as a model to grow more disciples by paving the way for the Gospel to be spread to and fro the ends of the Earth!

Now do not get me wrong, God is certainly capable of performing the same sort of supernatural miracles today as he did in Jesus' time on Earth and through the Apostle's after the Holy Spirit came on them, which continues to authenticate His deity as it did then. However, the work that we have all been called on to carry out today is to proclaim the good news of the gospel of grace to a lost and dying world and to show the world Love as Jesus Loved us - as is said in John 6:29; *"THIS is the work of God, that you believe in Him Whom He has sent."*

And in that message, we must consider that "Love "One Another" could easily encompass the entire range of sayings as a general statement of how to act towards each other. After all, Jesus essentially consolidated fulfillment of all 10 commandments in the form "Love God and love your neighbor" as found in Mark 12:30-31. Loving our neighbor necessarily involves loving "One Another".

And fulfillment of "Love "One Another" certainly covers the remainder of the "One Another" Themes can be seen as expressions of love, or the outward working of these love relationships in different situations. In fact, the other themes could really be subsets of the larger set titled "love" and the reason we began with what I have found to be the foundation for Christian living and the themes of "One Another" Love, Unity, Humility & Servanthood, and Encouragement & Edification.

If you think about it, they are all essentially expressions of Love and how to Love "One Another".

HUMILITY & SERVANTHOOD

When I visualize Humility & Servant hood, I truly imagine a tapestry with each fiber interwoven together to produce a single and incredibly important characteristic of a follower of Christ!

Thinking back to again those final hours before Jesus was to be seized and put to death, he exhibited both in parallel which I believe to some degree they go hand in hand! In John 13: 1-17, when Jesus removes his outer garment and washes the feet of his disciples, he exhibits both humility and servant hood especially since this in the Jewish custom was a task that a slave would normally perform for their masters.

But even more so washing the feet of Jesus' Disciples was not implicitly an act of humility but also symbolic of bringing the disciples to take part in his death and resurrection. You see, the Greek word *tithenai* which is used in this passage refers to Jesus laying aside His garments and is the same word used in the context of Jesus laying down His life for others, so in effect it was symbolic of inviting the disciples to share in his death and resurrection.

And as an act of servant hood and humility he demonstrated what we see in John 13:14-15 as he set the example for his disciples as John clearly conveys in his Gospel and account of the words spoken by Jesus below.

> 14 "Now that I, your Lord and Teacher, have washed your feet, you also should wash One Another's feet.
> 15 I have set you an example that you should do as I have done for you."

While nothing in comparison this reminds me of a time when the Lord pressed upon me the importance of serving and showed me what I have referred to for many years as the joy of serving. With the leading of the Holy Spirit, I humbly went before my Churches service ministry and when completing the form remember distinctly filling in use me as the Lord would have me.

At that time, I was still relatively new to my faith and quite frankly could not see where exactly I fit in so in obedience and a heart to please God and Love others as the one song says in the Lyrics, "I said Jesus Take the Wheel". At that time, I was trusted with little but over time the Lord took me on a journey of service that went in multiple directions and allowed me the honor of serving "One Another" (Galatians 5:13) and to do it humbly regarding "One Another" as more important than myself as the Apostle Paul conveys to the Church of Philippi in Philippians 2:3.

This then is the posture as Christians that we should have towards "One Another". As we share in Jesus' death, burial, and resurrection, Jesus expects us to take up our cross not just in suffering but in humble service as well. We are to put others first, and to cover ourselves with humility toward "One Another" as Peter has instructed us in 1 Peter 5:5.

As the body of Christ, we all have different gifts as the Apostle Peter said in 1 Peter 4:10 *As each has received a gift, use it to serve "One Another", as good stewards of God's varied grace*. Each of our gifts makes up Jesus' plan for the Church when they are used to serve "One Another" and do so with Humility! Our life of service and humility to "One Another" is our offering and part of our worship to God! *We do all this because we are in a real sense, members of "One Another"* as Paul establishes in 2 places; Romans 12:5 and Ephesians 4:25.

And while many of us might think that when the Scriptures says Whom the Son sets free is free indeed, they might be a bit surprised at the tall order that freedom comes with when you read what Paul has to say in Galatians 5:13; *You, my brothers and sisters, were called to be free. But do not use your freedom to indulge the flesh; rather, serve "One Another" humbly in love.*

So, as you begin to truly dive into the Bible there is so

much more as we are simply focusing on the verses that implicitly say "One Another" or in similar context "Each Other", it becomes clearer and clearer that a Christian's life of service is to "One Another" yet as unto the Lord! For after all as Hebrews 13:2 says, "*Do not forget to show hospitality to strangers, for by so doing some people have shown hospitality to angels without knowing it.*"

Therefore, I will leave you with one final nugget in this section from 1 Peter 4:10 where Peter tells us to: *Employ the gifts that God has given us for the benefit of "One Another"*. Or on a related and connected note as Jesus commands... "Love One Another".

ENCOURAGEMENT & EDIFICATION

Did you know that when you follow Christ your part in his Kingdom plan spans much broader than a nice little comfortable relationship with him! Even in our Churches, we are not just called to gather as if it were a social club but rather to not only train up believers but if I could compare this to a High School basketball team, we are there to spur each other on.

That is right, we work together like the cogs on a clock, we carry each other's burdens when we pick up where other teammates are struggling or need to make a pass. We huddle together with each time out to plan, to correct, and to encourage. Our coach who could be the equivalent of our Pastor or Mentor are on the sidelines training us up both on and off the court and ultimately, we are being trained to train up new players or in the case of Church New Believers for the Kingdom to go and spread the Good News.

When I think of this, I recall what the Apostle Paul says in 1 Thessalonians 5:11 as he tells us; "*Therefore encourage "One Another" and build each other up, just as in fact you are doing.*"

That is right, we have, and this is just one example and by command from Christ himself or through the anointed messages of the Holy Spirit through the Apostles have an obligation to equip the Saints and it is foundational that in order to do this we understand the need for "One Another". In other Words, we have a responsibility and are not to take it lightly to come alongside our brothers and sisters in Christ and both Encourage and Edify them!

Webster's defines edify as a transitive verb which is a type of action verb that links the subject with the object or in the case of the Bible's use of another brother or sister in Christ! The Word means to instruct and improve especially in moral and religious knowledge, to uplift, enlighten, and inform.

Romans 14:19 really hits home on how caring Christians encourage and edify "One Another" and in short that is congruent with how they Love "One Another". We have already looked at and emphasized the "One Another" theme of LOVE". Loving "One Another" is not only a matter of words; it is a matter of deeds, or more precisely said Love is an action. It is one thing to say to someone, "I love you," but quite notably different to prove it by our actions. Let us refocus on the word "edify" which we just spoke about but this time in verse 19 of Romans Chapter 14.

Similar in wording but same in context the word means "to build up" which is a good way of summarizing how Webster's defines it! It comes from the Latin word which means "to build." Christians who care and I might also say obey since many of the references in scripture are from a posture of a command; edify "One Another".

They encourage and they build "One Another" up in the faith and come along them so that they both grow and do not stumble. And when they do stumble, they gently correct or edify and help them to get back up on their feet again! The Lord has called us to be used to help "build up" others, or on the contrary because of free will, selfish desires, and our inability to Love also to be used by Satan to tear down, hurt, and to destroy the very people we are called to Love. It is much easier to be a critic or destroyer than to be a vessel of positive and life-giving words and encouragement.

But it should not be so hard at least not if we are abiding in Christ Jesus and his high calling to Love "One Another" as "I Have Loved You", for God has given us a Spiritual toolkit for us to use for building up "One Another" and growing in Christ together as one body! We will break these tools into 5 thematic groups: Our Witness, Our Words, Our Spiritual Gifts & Talents, Our Love, and Our Prayers.

Our Witness

For our first theme in the chapter of Encouragement and Edification, we will turn to the writings of the Apostle Paul in Romans 14 verses 14 through 21 to see what the Bible has to say as it related to "One Another" how our witness, mannerism, and conduct play a role in the plans of God for his Children!

Romans 14:14-21

> *14 My union with the Lord Jesus makes me certain that no food is of itself ritually unclean; but if you believe that some food is unclean, then it becomes unclean for you.*
>
> *15 If you hurt others because of something you eat, then you are no longer acting from love. Do not let the food that you eat ruin the person for whom Christ died!*
>
> *16 Do not let what you regard as good get a bad name.*
>
> *17 For God's Kingdom is not a matter of eating and drinking, but of the righteousness, peace, and joy which the Holy Spirit gives.*
>
> *18 And when you serve Christ in this way, you please God and are approved by others.*

> *19 So then, we must always aim at those things that bring peace and that help strengthen "One Another".*
>
> *20 Do not, because of food, destroy what God has done. All foods may be eaten, but it is wrong to eat anything that will cause someone else to fall into sin.*
>
> *21 The right thing to do is to keep from eating meat, drinking wine, or doing anything else that will make other believers fall.*

Now, even though the word edify is not used in the NIV version, which is the translation I chose to use, the principles here and in the KJV's verse one says "receive ye" and in verse 19 we find edify "One Another". On a related note, we are instructed in verse 13 not to judge, which is in the context of unrighteous judgment. While the NIV and other more current translations do not specifically use the Words edify and "One Another" the same meaning comes from the phrase; "help strengthen "One Another".

So, now that we have some context from using the two translations, as you read through the scriptures you should be able to see how Paul is instructing us not to be a "Stumbling Block!" And to give further depth and understanding of what a stumbling block might be in the final verse he states what was not the obvious in the

Jewish custom and that being that all food or drink are good, but if our consumption would cause someone else to fall into sin then we should avoid when in their presence.

Now that does not mean that for example our responsible consumption of alcohol is a sin, but rather the point being our doing it might cause someone who struggles with alcohol moderation to backslide, trip up, and even in shame of falling short flat out run from the things of God!

I recall a time just a couple years ago when I invited a young lady that the Lord had laid on my heart to join me at Church! When we discussed dress, she asked me about our dress code. While my Church was quite comfortable in jeans including the Pastors, the Spirit brought this Scripture to mind and I wore a jacket, button down shirt to be sure that the young lady who was at that time convinced anything less was dishonoring God, would not give place to the Devil and decide not to go to Church due to offence!

Now, did I dress up because I thought it made me closer to God or that dressing in my normal attire would be a sin? No, of course not! But I did dress up to be sure that God's will would be done and so she would join me for Church and my dress would not be a "Stumbling Block".

So, by being a stumbling block the Bible is telling us we are partaking in an action that hurts or discourages another. Again, it does not mean it is wrong but if we are called to encourage then we encourage even if it is meeting someone where they are, so they are comfortable and heading towards and growing in the things of God!

By this we are setting an example of a Christian mature in their union with Christ is mindful of what Paul shares here as it leads us to encourage the weaker Christian to grow. And then God uses our Christian example as a means for edifying the other or "One Another".

Our Words

Now our second theme comes much for as the Scriptures say, "Out of the Tongue Comes Life and Death", or more precisely as said in Proverbs 18:21 in the Good News Translation; "What you say can preserve life or destroy it; so, you must accept the consequences of your words."

There is so much power in our words hence the reason the Bible says the tongue cannot be trained but with Jesus we know that it can be controlled and in order to truly have a "One Another" Gospel it is imperative that we are mindful in what we say for words as a Christen song goes can build you up, words can tear you down, put a fire in your heart, or put it out!

So we see why so many scriptures from Old Testament to New Testament speak about the tongue because it is in combination with our right or wrong thoughts responsible for the very things we say and whether or not those words encourage or discourage, edify or tear down.

In Ephesians 4:29, the Apostle Paul tells us, and this is in the context of a command to *"Not use harmful words, but only helpful words, the kind that build up and provide what is needed, so that what you say will do good to those who hear you."*

This is because as we speak to "One Another", we are either using words that build them up or tear them down. We need to actively and intentionally choose our words wisely and use words that encourage, edify, build up, and strengthen each other rather than words that cut like a knife, create division, and cause discouragement.

As brothers and sisters in Christ we are called to speak the truth in love and I think (Ephesians 4:15) in the Good News Translation gives the act of speaking the truth in Love full Character as it states, *"Instead, by speaking the truth in a spirit of love, we must grow up in every way to Christ, who is the head."* Yes, Paul is telling us to do this by the leading of the Spirit and reflects how our action of Love and gentle correction show our Spiritual maturity in Christ Jesus! As we speak the truth in love, we can build people up and we reflect the essence of Christ whose mercy has been extended to us and we are likewise called to extend it to "One Another".

Now Jesus knew this world would be harsh and I believe even he knew its harshness would pull on us, so I love the illustration he uses in Matthew 10:16 when Jesus says; *"Listen! I am sending you out just like sheep to a pack of wolves. You must be as cautious as snakes and as gentle as doves."* Sounds brutal doesn't it? Much of what we face as Christians is verbal persecution so if they are to know us as his followers our very words must align with them knowing us by our love!

And furthermore with "One Another", *"5 Be wise in the way you act toward those who are not believers, making good use of every opportunity you have."* and *"Our speech should always be pleasant and interesting, and you should know how to give the right answer to everyone." as Paul conveys in* Colossians 4:5-6. While the Phrase "One Another" is not specifically used in context to whom Paul is writing to he is clearly talking to the Church and if you continue on with the verses that follow you will see the very essence of community or "One Another"!

To wrap up this theme of Encouragement & Edification let us look at just a handful of additional Scriptures that instruct us how to use our words wisely! While there are many more, this should give you a foundation of apologetics to begin to dive in and read the Word for yourself and let the Spirit within you guide you to a life of Christian living that is pleasing to the Lord!

Proverbs 11:12-13

12 "It is foolish to speak scornfully of others. If you are smart, you will keep quiet. 13 No one who gossips can be trusted with a secret, but you can put confidence in someone who is trustworthy."

1 Thessalonians 5:11

11 "And so encourage "One Another" and help "One Another", just as you are now doing."

Hebrews 3:13

13 "Instead, in order that none of you be deceived by sin and become stubborn, you must help "One Another" every day, as long as the word "Today" in the scripture applies to us."

Our Spiritual Gifts & Talents

Because I like music and dancing, I will use this as an example for gifts & talents! I am sure if you have been a Christian for any length of time and if not, you will begin to understand that all good gifts come from God as you grow in your knowledge of the Lord!

God gives each of us unique gifts for glorifying him, edification of the church, and for serving "One Another"! So yes, that means as would be the case with me that my favorite 1980's rock bands received their talent from God even though many if not most were not and for those still around are not using their God given gifts for glorifying God and or edification of "One Another".

In fact, they may be using their gifts to purely satisfy the desires of the flesh or more accurately though perhaps in some cases stereotypic; "Drug, Sex, and Rock and Roll." So just because someone and it does not have to be a person or persons with a platform is not using their gifts for God's glory does not mean those gifts are not from him!

Or perhaps you are just a common man or woman who is incredibly talented at what you do in your career or a hobby. If you are for example painting pictures of evil, then you are likely not using your gifts for God. And even while there may be others who share your interest, it is only by deception that your use of your gift is truly breathing life into anyone.

So just as in 1 Corinthians 14:12 and 26 Paul first tells the Corinth Church who at that time was misusing their using their gifts much as I described the typical 1980's Rock Bands and not for building up or edifying "One Another".

So, in verse 12 the Apostle Paul is explaining to them because their eagerness to discover their gifts was also misleading their use of their gifts as he says in verse 12; *"Since you are eager to have the gifts of the Spirit, you must try above everything else to make greater use of those which help to build up the church."*

And then in verse 26 he instructs them on orderly use of their gifts within the Church by saying; *"This is what I mean, my friends. When you meet for worship, one person has a hymn, another a teaching, another a revelation from God, another a message in strange tongues, and still another the explanation of what is said. Everything must be of help to the Church."*

Did you catch that? "Everything must be of help to the Church" in which we cover that our gift should be edifying and in context since he is talking to the Church corporately and not as individuals since we are each the Church he is referencing in principal "One Another" again which you may be tired of hearing by now but is pivotal in truly understanding God's plan for the Gospel of Christ, the Kingdom of Heaven, and his Children in the here and now on Earth!

So, when we go to Church, we ought to have an attitude that is postured like Christ! We should be more concerned with what we can do for others than what we can get from others! We must sincerely pray for the Spirit to guide us in our gifts be they being on the Worship team, facilities, prayer, production, greeting and so on! We should be always conscious of the opportunity to help "One Another" grow, and to encourage and minister to "One Another" for edification, accountability and relationship!

Church should not be something we go to, it should be the very heart of who we are, and we should be eager to take the time to encourage others, speak words of encouragement, and not just rush in to get what we need and rush out. That would be like popping in for 10 minutes at a family get together and with exception being the case, our norm should be to spend quality time with our families and that is the same thing we are called to do as it pertains to the family of God!

Even though we have focused on New Testament I cannot help but include this verse from Isaiah 58:10 which so elegantly says; *"If you pour yourself out for the hungry and satisfy the desire of the afflicted, then shall your light rise in the darkness and your gloom be as the noonday."*

And then Matthew 10:8 which really drives home helping others and using our gifts as Jesus so boldly says to us; "Heal the sick, raise the dead, cleanse those who have leprosy, drive out demons. Freely you have received; freely give."

God shows us how to be generous givers through the examples of Scripture. As our closing example, Acts 9:36 says; *"Now there was in Joppa a disciple named Tabitha, which, translated, means Dorcas. She was full of good works and acts of charity."*

Our Love

As with the other parent themes in this book the theme of Love just as it will in the sub theme of Encouragement & Edification be the foundation for us a Christians to edify and build up our brothers and sisters in Christ.

Paul begins 1 Corinthians 8:1 saying, "*Now, concerning what you wrote about food offered to idols. It is true, of course, that all of us have knowledge, as they say. Such knowledge, however, puffs a person up with pride; but love builds up*"

So, there you have it "Love builds up". So, let us close in prayer! Not really but you should get my point that Paul takes no time getting straight to the point but we will continue to build on this just so we are certain you have a good foundation of Apologetics to build on yourself as you dive into the Word and learn the power of "One Another" in Christian Living!

So, as we continue and while we will come back to Paul on this topic let us see what Jesus had to say in Matthew 24:40 and just what he meant; "*The King will reply, 'I tell you, whenever you did this for one of the least important of these followers of mine, you did it for me!*"

Now the Bible is clear that nothing can separate us from the Love of God, we love and worship an invisible God. As you see even in the days of Moses, he has forbidden us to make an image of himself, for he is a jealous God. However, through Christ, he has put his image into mankind. If we would see him and serve him, we must see and serve our fellow man and 1 John repeatedly makes references to our Love and belief in God whom we have not seen to how we treat "One Another" who we have seen.

But beyond that, we must see and serve "the least of these"; for in this we can more intimately know that our service is rendered to God out of Love for him and for the Glory of God almighty. Serving those who are of worldly importance, especially those who can return the favor as mentioned in Luke 14:12, is not specifically wrong, but the motive for such service could always be in question, especially if the kind of service that Jesus is describing never occurs. And that is service that is to those who are even undeserving or hard to Love.

In the parable of the sheep and the goats, neither the sheep nor the goats expected the response of the master. The sheep are surprised that they were serving Christ by serving the least of these. The goats were surprised that they were failing Christ by failing the least of these. The goal here would be to do all things and render all service to all people for the glory of God and the sake of the Gospel.

Let us look at this parable together and see if we can come to a clearer understanding of what Jesus was conveying!

Matthew 25:31-46

The Sheep and the Goats

> 31 "When the Son of Man comes in his glory, and all the angels with him, he will sit on his glorious throne."

32 *"All the nations will be gathered before him, and he will separate the people one from another as a shepherd separates the sheep from the goats."*

33 *"He will put the sheep on his right and the goats on his left."*

34 *"Then the King will say to those on his right, 'Come, you who are blessed by my Father; take your inheritance, the kingdom prepared for you since the creation of the world.*

35 *"For I was hungry, and you gave me something to eat, I was thirsty, and you gave me something to drink, I was a stranger and you invited me in,"*

36 *"I needed clothes and you clothed me, I was sick, and you looked after me, I was in prison and you came to visit me."*

37 *"Then the righteous will answer him, 'Lord, when did we see you hungry and feed you, or thirsty and give you something to drink?"*

38 *"When did we see you a stranger and invite you in, or needing clothes and clothe you?"*

39 "When did we see you sick or in prison and go to visit you?"

40 "The King will reply, 'Truly I tell you, whatever you did for one of the least of these brothers and sisters of mine, you did for me."

41 "Then he will say to those on his left, 'Depart from me, you who are cursed, into the eternal fire prepared for the devil and his angels."

42 "For I was hungry, and you gave me nothing to eat, I was thirsty, and you gave me nothing to drink,"

43 "I was a stranger, and you did not invite me in, I needed clothes and you did not clothe me, I was sick and in prison and you did not look after me."

44 "They also will answer, 'Lord, when did we see you hungry or thirsty or a stranger or needing clothes or sick or in prison, and did not help you?"

45 "He will reply, 'Truly I tell you, whatever you did not do for one of the least of these, you did not do for me."

46 "Then they will go away to eternal punishment, but the righteous to eternal life."

Now this is Jesus' final teaching in this section and examines how we treat those in need. While the words sheep and goats are not explicitly mentioned in the text, they are metaphors that go hand and hand with the parable Jesus tells! In this account, when Jesus returns in his glory, he will sit on his throne and separate people "as a shepherd separates the sheep from the goats" as stated in Matthew 25:32.

The separation depends on how we treat people in need. To the sheep he says, these are all people in need, whom the sheep served, for Jesus says, "*Just as you did it to one of the least of these who are members of my family, you did it to me*" in Matthew 25:40.

To the goats, he says, individually and corporately AKA "One Another": we are called to help those in need. We are "bound in the bundle of the living under the care of the Lord our God, and we cannot ignore the circumstance of human suffering hunger, thirst, nakedness, homelessness, sickness, or imprisonment.

We are called to work in order to meet our own needs and the needs of those dependent on us; but we also called to work in order to have something to give to those in need as Hebrews 13:1-3 conveys.

Hebrews 13:1-3

> 1 "Keep on loving "One Another" as Christians."
>
> 2 "Remember to welcome strangers in your homes. There were some who did that and welcomed angels without knowing it."
>
> 3 "Remember those who are in prison, as though you were in prison with them. Remember those who are suffering, as though you were suffering as they are."

And what powerful messages that speaks so directly too many of the sub themes in Encouragement and Edification Chapter of this book is Chapter 4 of the Epistle 1 Peter! In 1 Peter 4 just to grab a few nuggets we are given the following directives from Peter, the Rock through whom Jesus built his Church on and who walked with Jesus intimately as did the other disciples!

1 Peter Chapter 4

> *1 Peter 4:8 "Above everything, love "One Another" earnestly, because love covers over many sins.*
>
> *1 Peter 4:8 "Open your homes to each other without complaining"*
>
> *1 Peter 4:7 "The end of all things is near. You must be self-controlled and alert, to be able to pray."*
>
> *1 Peter 4:10 "Each one, as a good manager of God's different gifts, must use for the good of others the special gift he has received from God."*

Again, while not every scripture I will reference in this book will specifically say "One Another" or "Each Other", when you read the verses in context to the writer's message there is no denying the call to the commands to live a life of service!

To Love "One Another" by being useful for the cause of the Kingdom and that Kingdom undoubtedly is a "One Another" Kingdom! And its message lives in the heart of our Savior's Words in his "One Another" Gospels.

Our Prayers

Can you imagine scourged, mocked, and now nailed to the cross bearing not just the weight of all past, present, and future sins for all mankind, Jesus still while gasping for his very next breath still uttered the words "Father, forgive them for they do not know what they are doing" are found in Luke 23:34.

Yes, Jesus who in his final moments was looking down from the cross and the crowds, many condemning, mocking, and even spitting on him had to have been distressing to Him. He stared as the Roman soldiers were gambling for His clothing as John accounts in his Gospel in Chapter 19:23–24. The criminals on the crosses to either side of Him were criticizing Him and the Pharisees and Sadducees were mocking Him as the Gospel of Matthew in Matthew 27:41–43 tells us. Even the crowd, many who had once followed him were blaspheming Him as accounted in Matthew 27:39.

But still, even though he was paying a price in his innocence and surrounded by the most unworthy groups of haters you can imagine, Jesus still prayed for them. "Father, forgive them" and to this writer this story, this truth, this depiction of LOVE, demonstrates why we are called to pray for "One Another" and even though they did not deserve it, he still prayed that he was willing to forgive those who would repent and have faith. Either then or before they breathed their last breath!

So, Jesus was willing to forgive them—forgiveness was, in fact, the reason He was on the cross. The words

"Father, forgive them" further show the merciful heart of God the Father, and the Love he had for us through the sacrifice which was Love in action when he sent his son into the world to pray for, teach, set the example, and eventually pay the debt for our sins. I pray that you can grasp the magnitude of the Father and the Sons Love to literally pray for us as we begin to look at the importance of prayer as exemplified by Jesus and the power praying for "One Another" has on edifying the brethren.

Just as we build each other up by our witness, our words, our spiritual gifts & talents, and our love we also build up "One Another" or edify "One Another" by our Prayers. As we pray for "One Another", then God can work and build them up for no prayer is left unanswered though to be clear God may answer our prayers very differently than we envision!

One of the first sets of verses that come to mind when I think about the emphasis on prayer in the Epistles comes from the book of James. In just four verses James virtually covers the spectrum of prayer for us and for "One Another"

James 5:13-16

> 13 "Are any among you in trouble? They should pray. Are any among you happy? They should sing praises."
>
> 14 "Are any among you sick? They should send for the church elders, who will pray for them and rub olive oil on them in the name of the Lord."
>
> 15 "This prayer made in faith will heal the sick; the Lord will restore them to health, and the sins they have committed will be forgiven."
>
> 16 "So then, confess your sins to "One Another" and pray for "One Another", so that you will be healed. The prayer of a good person has a powerful effect."

Since the general theme of this book is on the **"Power of One Another"**, let us home in on verse 16 for a moment! Not only is James telling us to confess our sins to "One Another", but he also tells us to PRAY for "One Another" and if that is not enough, he ads so we will be healed and then tops it off by what in some translations states; "The prayers of a righteous man avails much."

Even verse 15 is postured in a way that our prayers of faith for others will heal the sick for the Lord will restore them to health and the sins they have committed will be forgiven. Now of course repentance on the others part is a necessary component and how God chooses to heal is according to his will for that person these are powerful promises and examples of why it is important for us to pray for "One Another".

So, in conclusion, there are many more truths to this principle of Praying for "One Another" our prayers are used by God to build up His people! Christians who care 'love "One Another" and 'edify "One Another". If someone had to describe your walk with Christ, would they see the application of "One Another" in your life? Think about that!

CHAPTER 8

"ONE ANOTHER" DON'TS

I honestly think a good place that serves as an umbrella that the Bible speaks of in the context of "One Another" and how not to treat each other would be Paul's emphasis in Hebrew 10:25. In this passage he instructs us to not give up meeting together, as some are in the habit of doing, but rather he encourages us to regularly like weekly Church to interact or fellowship with "One Another", and as he adds; "and all the more as you see the Day approaching."

As believers in Christ, we are to be all about "One Another", so even some of the positives like preferring "One Another" or others over ourselves have a negative connotation when we put ourselves first and act in a selfish manner!

But homing in on the specifics that the bible uses a direct "One Another" or "each "other reference, we are instructed not to lie to "One Another", pass judgment on

"One Another", not to grumble with "One Another" and as if you would think we would not need to be told this but to stop biting and devouring "One Another" as conveyed in Galatians 5:15.

And, in Galatians we are instructed to provoke "One Another" and in James to not slander "One Another". Clearly you should be seeing a theme here that we cannot have Unity with "One Another", Love "One Another", exhibit Humility and Serve "One Another", or Encourage and Edify "One Another" if we are grumbling, slandering, lying to, cheating, etc. "One Another".

And as referenced in context I really think while all the "One Another" specifically tell us how to and how not to treat each other, as I said before in reverse or by not doing those that are especially those of a command, we are doing the opposite and growing the list on "One Another" don'ts! While it is not this writer's intention to insult his reader's intelligence and not be confident that you get the point, I would like to share one last verse. James in 4:11 which delivers a powerful and linked succession of do nots.

JAMES IN 4:11

> *"Do not slander "One Another".*
> *Anyone who speaks against his brother*
> *or judges him speaks against the law*
> *and judges it. When you judge the law,*
> *you are not keeping it,*
> *but sitting in judgment on it."*

CHAPTER 9

CHRISTIAN LIVING SUMMED UP AS "ONE ANOTHER"

I love the way Luke sums up what he set out to accomplish by writing the Gospel of Luke in the beginning of Acts 1:1-5. He begins with addressing Theophilus, his friend in which scholars believe was of high stature and Luke set out to write this 25-foot scroll to convey the events to him and leave a historical record to the world.

Acts 1:1-5

1 In my first book I wrote about all the things that Jesus did and taught from the time he began his work 2 until the day he was taken up to heaven. Before he was taken up, he gave instructions by the power of the Holy Spirit to the men he had chosen as his apostles.

3 For forty days after his death he appeared to them many times in ways that proved beyond doubt that he was alive. They saw him, and he talked with them about the Kingdom of God. 4 And when they came together, he gave them this order: "Do not leave Jerusalem, but wait for the gift I told you about, the gift my Father promised. 5 John baptized with water, but in a few days, you will be baptized with the Holy Spirit."

Luke tells us in his Gospel in Luke 1:1-3 that he collected information from eyewitnesses, and he carefully wrote what he heard in chronological order. Luke is the only writer who claims to have written in chronological order. The other gospels tend to be written in thematic order. Even though in those days it was thought to be less important to write Chronology. Scholars also believe he wrote the Gospel with gentiles as his primary audience so perhaps that might explain as he was giving them a historical account, since they had not grown-up hearing the accounts of Jesus passed down in conversations. However, that is merely an assumption of this writer.

So, moving back to the book of Acts and stepping forward in time a bit in the book of Acts and setting the stage for yet another account of Luke's yet one that he was not entirely written as would be the case of a "Cold Case Detective" or historian as he had many interactions with the Apostle Paul over the ladder part of Paul's life as a "Slave to Jesus Christ" as he often referred!

Now beginning with Luke's account and this per se was not one he experienced firsthand but did much later during Nero's reign and persecution of the Church, let us look at how the Church is described in Acts 2:43-47 and subtitled in the Good News Translation; "Life Among Believers".

Acts 2:43:47

> *3 Many miracles and wonders were being done through the apostles, and everyone was filled with awe.*
>
> *44 All the believers continued together in close fellowship and shared their belongings with "One Another".*
>
> *45 They would sell their property and possessions, and distribute the money among all, according to what each one needed.*
>
> *46 Day after day they met as a group in the Temple, and they had their meals together in their homes, eating with glad and humble hearts,*
>
> *47 praising God, and enjoying the good will of all the people. And every day the Lord added to their group those who were being saved.*

Let me call out a handful or two words and phrases in this short verse for us to focus on!

- Everyone
- Believers
- Together
- Close Fellowship
- Shared Their
- Sell Property
- Sell Possessions
- Each One Needed
- Met as a Group
- Meals Together
- Humble Hearts
- Praising God
- Enjoying Good Will
- Added to their Group
- Being Saved
- And of course… "One Another"

Just in this short five verse scripture one can easily see Jesus' plan for "One Another", "Community", and Christian Living! The deity of Christ and the exclusivity of Christ is what makes Christianity different. He is the one true God and the ONLY way to the Father. And who best would know how our lives needed to be structured then God almighty who put aside his deity and walked in the very shoes you and I do today when he came to dwell among us some 2000 plus years ago.

Another great example of God's plan for "One Another" can be found in both word and principal and depicts an excellent example of Christian Living in a "One Another" Gospel. Galatians Chapter six can be coined as the bearing of "One Another's" burdens! A biblical principle and command incorporated in this book "The Power of One Another"!

In fact, I find it so interesting that the author needs to tell us but after all we are a bit thick headed AKA stubborn at times that... "Do not be deceived: God is not mocked, for whatever one sows, that will he also reap" This immediately follows Paul's direct command to bear "One Another's" Burdens and correlates this with fulfilling the "Law of Christ"! Which we know by Christ himself and the many teachings especially of John that LOVE is the key to fulfillment of the law!

However, shifting to verse 9 we are also told to now give up on doing good! Now there is more but let us home in on that statement a little more before moving forward! We know that even in the Old Testament we are told to be Determined and of Courage! Deuteronomy 31:6 begins with "Be strong and of good courage!" and Joshua 1:9... "Have I not commanded you? Be strong and courageous" to name a couple!

Now verse 9 may actually be in fact metaphorically a "Name it and Claim" it scripture though true study of the Word of God reveals that this type of preaching is non scriptural. However in this case I think there is some truth to it as if we sow negatively we will in fact reap negatively and if we sow positively at minimum we will be rewarded in Heaven!

So if you are constantly tearing people down rather than uplifting them and caring only about yourself which is the opposite of how this verse starts then you will likely find over time you reap what you sow! If you are unkind to others they will likely be less likely to be kind to you, if you abuse those who you should Love you may lose what should have been dear to you just to name a few. For your Father in Heaven is watching and as the scripture says he will not be mocked.

Or in other words, "A person cannot claim to accept the gospel and the obligations that come with it and at the same time live in obedience to the flesh instead of the Spirit" (Ronald Y. K. Fung, The Epistle to the Galatians).

LUTER, A. B. (2017). GALATIANS. IN E. A. BLUM & T. WAX (EDS.), CSB STUDY BIBLE: NOTES (P. 1866). NASHVILLE, TN: HOLMAN BIBLE PUBLISHERS.

So remember Paul who says run the good race. Well that is because the Christian life is a marathon race, so let us not grow weary or lose heart. When we do good it is our goal to be justified by works, but rather to live as God has planned for those who have received his gracious salvation through faith. To "sow to the Spirit" over the long haul means taking the opportunity (Gk kairos, "opportune or appointed time") that the Lord places before us to work for the good of all.

And not only are we to work for the good of all, the Bible teaches us that believers are indwelled with the Holy Spirit, which is God's Spirit, but that we are also saved by Grace and Faith in Christ as our Lord and Savior. But not only did He save us from eternal death, He proclaimed how our identity would be known to the world in his Word by saying, "If you have Love for "One Another", then everyone will know that you are my disciples." in John 13:35.

As we are His and truly live-in unity with Jesus and live the Christian life, we die to self to live a life by faith. Just as Paul told the Galatians in Galatians 2:20, "*I have been crucified with Christ and I no longer live, but Christ lives in me. The life I live in the body, I live by faith in the Son of God, who loved me and gave himself for me*". Being crucified with Christ means that we consider our old nature as having been nailed to the cross and we choose to live in the new nature, which is Christ's (2 Corinthians 5:17).

He who loved us and died for us now lives in us, and the life we live is by faith in Him. Living the Christian life means sacrificing our own desires, ambitions, and glories and replacing them with those of Christ. We can only do this by His power through the faith that He gives us by His grace. Part of the Christian life is praying to that end.

And as we have learned in this book Christ himself,

the Apostles who walked with him, and the Apostle Paul whose life was turned inside out on the road to Damascus, have all written book after book, the ultimate owner's manual, the ultimate book of LOVE, and the premise and foundational importance of "One Another" as we seek to follow Jesus our example who gave it all on the way to and on the cross for each and every one that would believe and would receive his selfless gift of LOVE and sacrifice for the good of others or as simply said for "One Another".

So, in closing, let us not ever lose sight of the high calling of Unity, Love, Humility, Servanthood, Encouragement, and Edification Jesus Christ who reconciled us to our Father God has laid out for us in his Word so that we may live the Christian life for the good of "One Another" and the glory of our King and Savior Jesus Christ our Lord!

And remembering the Words from 1 John 4:7-21 which we will end with, truly embrace the message of Love and while the phrase "One Another" is not used, se how the message John reminds us of and the message Jesus commanded us to hours before he was taken in the captivity to begin what he had been destined and born to do and embrace God's message of Love and how we are to Love One Another and how that looks through God's lenses.

God Is Love

7 Beloved, let us love one another, for love is from God, and whoever loves has been born of God and knows God. 8 Anyone who does not love does not know God, because God is love. 9 In this the love of God was made manifest among us, that God sent his only Son into the world, so that we might live through him. 10 In this is love, not that we have loved God but that he loved us and sent his Son to be the propitiation for our sins. 11 Beloved, if God so loved us, we also ought to love one another. 12 No one has ever seen God; if we love one another, God abides in us and his love is perfected in us.

13 By this we know that we abide in him and he in us, because he has given us of his Spirit. 14 And we have seen and testify that the Father has sent his Son to be the Savior of the world. 15 Whoever confesses that Jesus is the Son of God, God abides in him, and he in God. 16 So we have come to know and to believe the love that God has for us. God is love, and whoever abides in love abides in God, and God abides in him. 17 By this is love perfected with us, so that we may have confidence for the day of judgment, because as he is so also are we in this world. 18 There is no fear in love, but perfect love casts out fear. For fear has to do with punishment, and whoever fears has not been perfected in love. 19 We love because he first loved us. 20 If anyone says, "I love God," and hates his brother, he is a liar; for he who

does not love his brother whom he has seen cannot love God whom he has not seen. 21 And this commandment we have from him: whoever loves God must also love his brother.

ONE ANOTHER INDEX

As we discussed in the book there are both positive and negative One Another phrases with characteristics on how to treat One Another and how not to treat One Another! A comprehensive list follows for your reference as you dive into the Word of God.

POSITIVE COMMANDS
How to treat One Another!

Love one another (John 13:34 - This command occurs at least 16 times)

Be devoted to one another (Romans 12:10)

Honor one another above yourselves (Romans 12:10)

Live in harmony with one another (Romans 12:16)

Build up one another (Romans 14:19; 1 Thessalonians 5:11)

Be like minded towards one another (Romans 15:5)

ONE ANOTHER INDEX

Accept one another (Romans 15:7)

Admonish one another (Romans 15:14; Colossians 3:16)

Greet one another (Romans 16:16)

Care for one another (1 Corinthians 12:25)

Serve one another (Galatians 5:13)

Bear one another's burdens (Galatians 6:2)

Forgive one another (Ephesians 4:2, 32; Colossians 3:13)

Be patient with one another (Ephesians 4:2; Colossians 3:13)

Speak the truth in love (Ephesians 4:15, 25)

Be kind and compassionate to one another (Ephesians 4:32)

Speak to one another with psalms, hymns and spiritual songs (Ephesians 5:19)

Submit to one another (Ephesians 5:21, 1 Peter 5:5)

Kindness and compassion for one another (Philippians 2:1)

Consider others better than yourselves (Philippians 2:3)

Look to the interests of one another (Philippians 2:4)

Bear with one another (Colossians 3:13)

Teach one another (Colossians 3:16)

Comfort one another (1 Thessalonians 4:18)

Encourage one another (1 Thessalonians 5:11)

Exhort one another (Hebrews 3:13)

Concerned for one another (Hebrews 10:24)

Help one another (Hebrews 10:24)

Show hospitality to one another (1 Peter 4:9)

Employ the gifts that God has given us for the benefit of one another (1 Peter 4:10)

Clothe yourselves with humility towards one another (1 Peter 5:5)

Pray for one another (James 5:16)

Confess your faults to one another (James 5:16)

NEGATIVE COMMANDS
How not to treat One Another

Do not lie to one another (Colossians 3:9)

Stop passing judgment on one another (Romans 14:13)

If you keep on biting and devouring each other...you'll be destroyed by each other (Galatians 5:15)

ONE ANOTHER INDEX

Let us not become conceited, provoking and envying each other (Galatians 5:26)

Do not slander one another (James 4:11)

Don't grumble against each other (James 5:9)

We do all this because we are in a real sense "members of one another" (Romans 12:5; Ephesians 4:25)

www.ingramcontent.com/pod-product-compliance
Lightning Source LLC
Chambersburg PA
CBHW071836290426
44109CB00017B/1833